THE WILDFIRE.

ABID MASROOR SHAH

Made with ♥ on the Notion Press Platform
www.notionpress.com

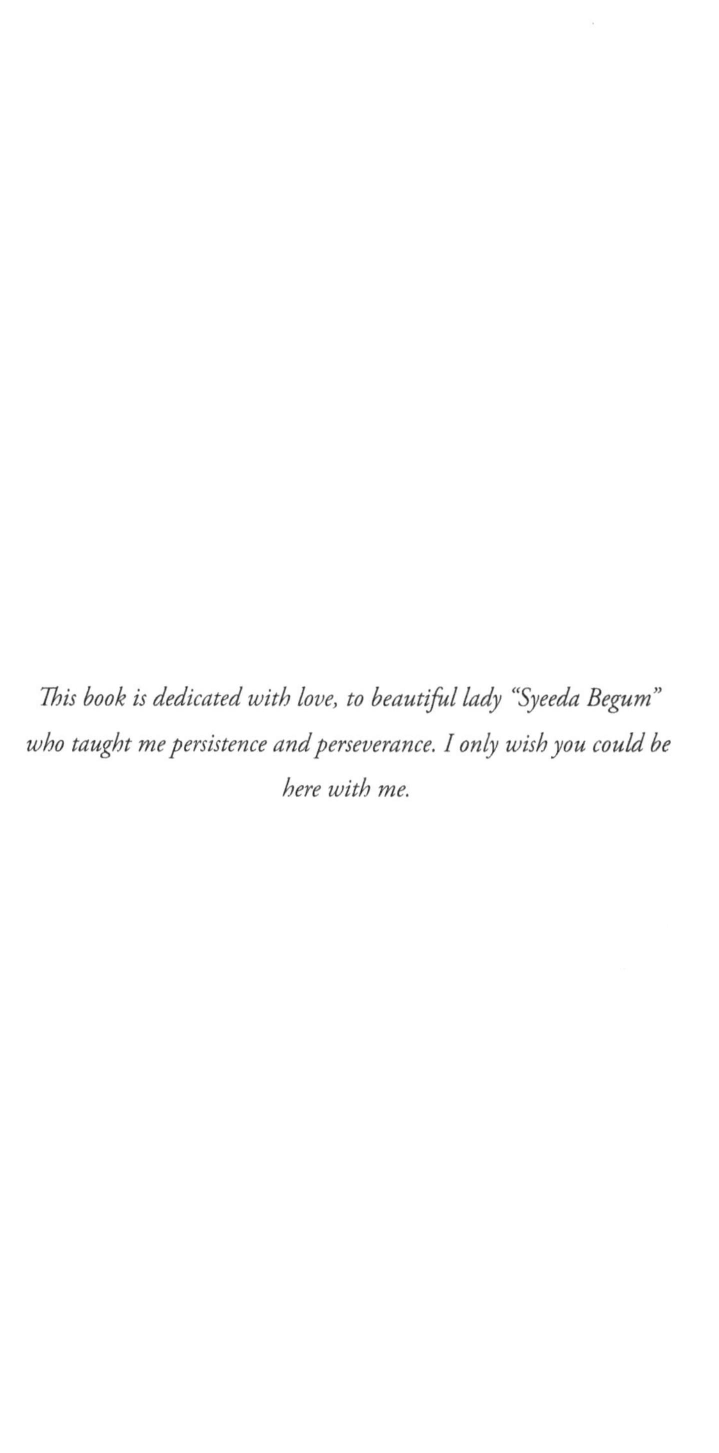

This book is dedicated with love, to beautiful lady "Syeeda Begum" who taught me persistence and perseverance. I only wish you could be here with me.

Contents

Contents

Contents

The Wildfire.

By:

Abid Masroor Shah.

E-mail:- aabidmasroor101@outlook.com

E-book:- http://www.poemhunter.com/aabid-masroor/

Linkedin:-https://www.linkedin.com/in/abid-masroor-shah-27720b1ab/

Qoute

Then what could death do when I depart
And when there is empty chamber of heart
Hath no fear to loose, no one to recall
Hath no pains to choose, no one to fall.

<u>Abid masroor.</u>

Foreword

This collection of poems is imaginative handiwork influenced by nature, love ,pathos ,environment , and day to day life happenings around. The currents of imagination and deep thinking are visible and can be equally felt by the reader. The mood of the author is more philosophical. Most of the poems are holy poems they speak of love towards God, concept of God.

There are poems which have some rhyme schemes, most of the poems are blank verses and most of them are rhythmic. The diction of the poems show that the poet is highly imaginative. Understanding of the poems provides the under current of the feelings and emotions and above all the message conveyed there in.

Message

Abid Masroor is a young promising poet, tries to present human condition in dilemma. Through his artistic skill he finds solution in universal love and brotherhood. The alienation which is because of materialistic pursuits can be done away by inculcating noble traits and positive thinking within ourselves. Love, piety benedictions are the worthwhile virtues, as the young poet believes in.

"He deserves all encouragement and appreciation."

Prof. Zahida Naseem.
H.O.D English Department.
S.P College 2013.

A Word About The Author

The collection of poems is a creative work of a young boy of 23 years of age. Though young in age yet matured in imagination. The creative instinct in him has developed when he was a school boy. He has all along been imaginative, expressive, narrative, sentimental and philosophical.

His collection of poems is superb with respect to idea, theme, and diction. They convey a message of love

He is influenced by nature, environment around him, happenings going on here and there whether favorable or unfavorable .

The number of poems that he has composed at this stage speak of his vastness of ideas and forecast of his future magnitude.

> *"I wish his growth and success in years to come."*

G.M.D Shaheen.
October, 24,2015.

"Mr **Abid Masroor** is pursuing his higher studies in Computer Science at the PG Department of Computer Science ,North Campus of Kashmir University ,but his heart is rooted in delicate emotions and feelings.He speaks and breathes love in his poems that are about man ,God and nature. Though all the time dealing and working with mechanical life of computer machines ,this young budding poet of our state promises a great talent that might someday unravel the deepest mysteries of human nature ,human yearning for the unknown and human aspirations for the God. I am glad to see the young author publishing his maiden collection of poetry as I believe these free strokes of thought and emotions that he has committed to paper will for sure lead him on the path of becoming a great master of the genre some day. A poet is supposed to have a good command on language ,have a good imagination and of course the content of thoughts and feelings to deal with in his/her writings.Mr Aabid seems to promise all the three ,though he needs a lot of hard work and dedication for a better work in future.

"I wish him all the best and request him to keep it up!"

Dr.Ameen Fayaz.
English Department.
University of Kashmir 2016.

As for Abid, he is pleasant to be interact with anyone. He is spontaneous in writing poem about anything, such a natural poet and his poetry skills are very impressive and unique. It is proud to have you as a friend.

> *"Hey man, My heartiest congratulations to take a step into domestic life. I appreciate your talent keep writing and never get distracted."*

Ajanthan Antony.
Tech Specialist - Network Operations.
AT&T.

1. To love

The moon on its silent road,
That hides in cloud whiz
There is silence in your woods
The owl , the walnut tree
In same aesthetic form, used to be.

The wind clamant this whirring sound tonight
Again currents shall toss from coast to coast
From your heart, I am aware of
This secret seclusion,
Delicately there will be no-connection

And you may meet another traveler
Butterflies ,rainbows, a new Inimitable hope,
You may not hesitate like used to…
Since I will be long gone
You will sing other love-song

2. Master of secrets

There is no God, there is no lord
Somebody said just
Illusive thoughts, concepts like resurrection
There is no certain fine perfection

There is no symbol, there is no sign
There is no, guide line
World is ours cheer with in
Who will seek commit a sin
Verify: O disbeliever . . .
For what is he created?
From what is he created?
None from drop emitted
He beholds powers unlimited

Don't you see the vastness of sky?
What makes it stand alone?
Floating and Passing clouds by
Bring downpour above from high

In the thickets, on the mountains
In the meadows, on the barren
In the vale's on the hill stations
And on the hotbeds of plantations

HE-The Lord of moons
HE-The Master of hidden thoughts
From every matter that I may find
HE-The Sustainer of mankind.

3. Love that

Love and to be loved is probability
When she says I love you
Gentle breeze whisper world is new
Love that, is expected,give itself back
Love no Agape-But
Something discrete and unpredictable,
Is not love at all
Love that, undivided-Can't be into two's
Can't be in flavor, taste, relative
Love that, total dedication,
Freedom, devotion, attention
Bounding foundation of truths

Love that, holds conformity between mind
And expected love in return
Love that, begins with strong feelings
Ends with casts, religions
Judgments, decisions, demands
Illusions, promises, priorities, options
Lies, selfishness, anger, negations
Negation is the failure of agreement

Leads to indeterminacy
Love that, not a game
A policy, a trick ,a scheme
What is it that make it to float on
Chaos, paradoxes and perplexities?
Love that, but is give and take
Where units speak of its oneness
Love that, being as
One, true, loyal, beautiful when
She says I hate you she means
Take her hand and don't look back
Love that love of God and love towards God
Act of pure giving without self benefit
Love that nothing is sought in return
What then-Is another name for love
love and to be loved is probability?

4. Spring

Flowers and sorrows, arise, gloom and die
Seasons, how can they twist knife in the cut
A full summer died in my arms but, the spring
When freezing bough of months came back to alive
But floating corpse-Alive what for
Birds- they don't join and sing a song
Those tones are rare, left with few
Drops on my face

The woods and mighty falls-sleep in rest
Seems winter is on its way
And spring smiled to me, said
Cuts and wounds bind within days
Dark of December is not with you always

5. If you, I fall again

If you, I fail again -fall again ,
In winter, in autumn or in rain
Spring- at no times came all the way
For twirling butterfly never they stay
I no longer chase the dancing leaves
Mine are but snow wintery eves
Where they lost in your dive
I am dead ,I am alive

6. Instead of

Moods and minds, winds and times
Fluctuate, as are you in old days
Of weak and full of sleep
The days of rest, the days of full of time
Time to read, in the deep, where silence creeps
To fill the same old air, into your lungs
As autumn waves from sky drifts
Windswept your mind and your cold nights
That blows and, blows
Leaves on the ground, memories all around
And then you will think of a book to read
That you will go to the libraries, instead of temples
You will happen to pass poetry section,
Instead of religious material
Oh, may you pick the same book
Wrote by the same lover ,there will be
My pages, instead of string beads
My lines, instead of holy verses

7. Who said that to you?

Less beautiful who said that to you?
When the hearts fail, her beauty made
Silent killing I should say, with open and
Awakening deep pointed lightning fire of eyes
In terror of, poets and innocents would die
Poets but I know not how they escape

Her face fairest, one some delay, it would have taken
To carve the eyebrow drawn above the white cheek
Upon her a careless smile pulse would break
Ever but none dare to gaze red lips that never mute
He would have been jealous

Cause if seasons, you were June
Gold beauteous to all trees
If a flower then you are a daffodil
Fresh fragrance to the glooms and blooms
If a winter then you are snow
That melt down and hesitate when you walk

If a spring then you are morning sun
That rises upon far hills bring back life for some cause
If a night then you are a dream
Of world well knows there, you and me, and me and you.
Less beautiful who said that to you?

"**<u>Dedicated to Eemaan Amin.</u>**"

8. Have I been fool by blossom and bloom?

Mighty fall of vapour from I belong
Uprear the eye almost the clearer high
In such sort the deep horizon
I fly over the great cloud
On the same wet green carpet
Grasp me and kissed the feet
Turn back and the footprints and the fancies
And another frost of woe to the land
Of a love it once belong
Of a voices that last song
Upon those grew a selfish nature's call
Cloud and eclipse to the sun and to the moon
And to the mind, and to the heart
Have I been fool by blossom and bloom?
Or forced to such do hang
Where none the false reflect
On the ashes of love sweet birds sang
The land expired which I take forth
Before the golden days

9. Tonight

Tonight from the dark vast horizon
Tonight from the bloodshed season
Tonight from the radiant frost
Tonight from the hope lost
Tonight from the no peace around
Tonight from the thunder sound
Tonight from the stars no gleaming
Tonight from the dark steep streaming
Tonight from the murdered moon
Tonight from the blind meets me soon
Tonight from the own heart alone
Tonight from the winds, direction unknown
Tonight from the temporary dream of child
Tonight from the voices of mean and wild
Tonight from the light of lightning
Tonight from the rain of pain
I saw
Her deep ocean blue eyes
Just reflecting some pain
It may be rain of sorrow tonight
It may be death of love tonight

10. (Love song)

Sometimes, long somehow
Near the flowing river, bend so wide
Curves behind the tree that grow upon
That bank to touch the smooth love currents
In the calm full moon light and let
Her come to me, somehow
In my fairyland, where I shall grow old with you let
Her come to me, somehow
How I wish this soft evening breeze
When drift from your land, your fragrance shed
To the same on my land, O let
Her come to me, somehow
But of my heart a solitary place
Where winds drove me, none is there let
Her winds gently pass by
Out of clouds that bursts into heavy rain and
My all love cuts away oft to see you
Like my heart your heart cuts away oft to see me and
Left home to meet in the romantic season let
Her come to me, somehow

11. Doleful planet

O' woe to disobedience
Made first
Of that restricted tree
Whose nasty taste
Brought chaos and graves
Into world
Made and fill with
Void and dire
Alas! Single baffle and bereavement
Seems as original brightness
Snatched
Obscured when sun reborn
Found through dubious
Horizontal effected air
Inglorious state
Dark designs of its own
Eclipsed and barren lands
Full of false filled with
Dusky, evil, wild, void souls
In their minds, regions of deep sorrow
Don't know itself is place can make
Hell of heaven, heaven of hell

12. When I saw you in the middle of the shore

When I saw you in the middle of the shore
If ever perfect landing how free
With the same I wonder by "IF"
The journey lifted by favorable winds
And the direction beyond the core
Under the blue careless floor
To touch the hidden secrets of sea
To bend the hope lesser than the vapour drop
Define in me in the middle of sea that sad reality
Which on earth and life of sea doth be one
I was not sailor of myths like but peace
Two in yours one in me and one is HE
Same the dream one fair journey It could be
The shore and the sailor let mingled be

13. Differences and Distances

Broke the heart with no fear
May be sensitive my dear
Act comfortable and hear
That? Take care is rare
Agree playing games with me
Many times not even three
I could have died may be
Into the desert, into the sea
I am a star with no light
Sun with no bright
Day with no night
Dream with no sight
Found myself. . .
Broken Lost in depth of love
Voices inside told me should I?
Should I not walk with the wide hopes
Struggling in an ocean all alone
Is that we call _love
No land near seaside and cove…?

Wish I could have a wish
On death of bed i
Woe to see into your eyes
Let me show you
Shape of my heart
Oh that last breathes
Let you be kind on me
Be the one in the last ceremony
Oh _that calm death
My pieces, my bones
None but _mark of stones
Solitary and differences
Wild winds and desert storms
Can't bear different forms
Differences and Distances I behold
Gold in copper mended and mold

14. Uncertainty

Deep inside vale, poor flower
Standing on stalk, oh land of clever
Beauty- All fallen to pieces
Petals tossed by storm fierce

That upcoming bud...
Welcome with grave frost and flood
Brought with him into the garden of blood
Scarce in years, negative obey
Harsh climate- no life, no day
Let it grow...

On the mountain of sorrow
On the risks of tomorrow
On the land of mystery
On the grave of history
And
Height to raise without fears
I have watched from years
Winter-winter for me and for all

No blooms and mighty river fall
Is that. . .
Vale, but kind of prison
Caged flower, no changing season
Spider life, web of foe
And no blossoms on the bough

15. Age that is dead

On the middle of palm, into the colorful waste land
Drink the poison of present, bear that in
Where devil rule the Gods land
And his son's aye the lines made
With the glory , honour and pride and praise
I will not govern down as if HE says
Or may it not be able to, but
How of lords direct the sun
As from east as from west is not the castles in the air
Is that of you can? but chained by opinion itself
O how let me in hawk's claws
Took me to the waves of white skies evil up top
Where I stood the age but not of mine
To see the time is there no time to wear
Endless civilization of machines and medicines
Of noble beings oft found doomed and replaced
O in what generation came it to me
Out seen wide open are wolves to justices
Even gave up when walked in the last
As it cuts my throat force to ancient pasts
Where sorrows least I find , reality stirs the mind
Beauties are born without odds

Of there eye wide open love and care
Days my love that glorious days
Flies and moths and butterflies more bright
On back of horse I could run miles apart
To the green, to the wild
Nights I spend in woods infrastructure of nests
More among the stars still can I count
Birds of miracle lines return to the same homeland
When the ocean welcome to the setting sun
When the grandmother cuddles me after story tell
A flower upon age that is dead

16. Awaken conscience

From the day of awaken conscience
Through mist have I passed
Down and far looking askance
Speck of dust
Sea of galaxies
Saw the garden ground
Treacherous glance
Testify . . .
There is God around for pure eye
And from heart there is fear
As I am not deaf, dumb and blind
I could see things
I could feel it

17. His birth

That companions and my companions of age
Ahh drops-in-desert
Poisoned by time, best healer they say- but what if,
Time is a disease infects precious holy teachings?
Bright majestic light one could differentiate from, and
Senseless wars what based on
Teachings it boldly face sandstorms time to time
It was not tale of Arabian nights, Alibaba, and Aladdin
Ease digested when
Delicious foods and primes welcome
It was not melodious music as you think over of it from dawn to
dusk
Gold's, diamonds and luxuries, welcome by
Was it a magic? That amaze more than a beautiful girl
what warm welcome it was
As weapon to the world of wars fond of
Hath left the desert and pieces of land
To be the battle field
Hath done the world rule by some ungodly dark
Oasis of desert or chosen sand
Good was born on the same desert of reptiles
To the same either black or white

THE WILDFIRE.

His birth was birth of light
Light with vacant skies went blue
Oft making rainbow colors
Bowing down moon a playing toy His birth
Was the birth of oneness
Birth of brotherhood, birth of mankind
Message of love truth and right
That He alone is designer up top
What then-a welcome by stones

18. With you (song)

So this is who I am
I carry you with me
So this is who I was
Went mute, broken for no cause

With you my land was free
As vast as ocean by
Where no harm could befall
Where flowers and mighty river fall

With you my days were bright
Cool breeze, blossom , golden sights
Shielded by mountain from every side
As mother embrace, cuddle her child

With you _Oh my poem, the moist breeze of ideas
Had left me all about you
Took me high as stars above
Filled my heart with lust and love

With you when flowers smelled
The soft breeze would pass by
Spring has come again with arise
My days are paradise

With you I was a complete man
Would differentiate loss and gain
Without you I die and cry
Dear don't say good bye

19. Lofted and disturbed

Lofted and disturbed
Seated lost in depth
Brooding on vast concept
Not day dealing tasks of my own
But habitually as regular fashion
Lofted off and disturbed

By fellow fanatically roaming
On paths of village
Surrounding there by folk
Laughing as he is a joke

No one knows his falsities
What makes him brittle?
What makes him pass away?
What makes him floating body?
What was his fault?

Once great warrior he was
Fond of blood and fight
Leader of mighty host
Strong muscles, smart as blaze
Close designer, work as guile
Day and night never he rest
Time passed caught in nest

THE WILDFIRE.

Surrounded with troops all over
Always heavy weapon bearer
Tricked by own one
Was rudely tortured
On that hit his mind
Lofted off and disturbed
By fellow fanatically roaming

20. Take my word

This love will be the death to me
How frazzle do I travel on the freeze
Though not ease recast not repose
The left that left me
Waved with me to woe
As if by some needle
Beastly burnt into my breast
And heavily hit by love's gravity
So of you my beauteous flower
Played me such a deep thorns
False breeze of petals, but sweet flowers do not
Of their fragrance beauty and bounty would arise
Of their promises hell seems paradise
Pour not the heart, my dear
When mine is full
I death my days, I slain my soul
As not myself mind was driven
For one sharp gaze one would freeze
But when in the time heaven behold
like in vale mighty vapour of river fall
Flowers kissed by butterflies beside
And in greenery - like a child lie

Simmered that land of fancies
To love that fair on the ashes
Take my word don't know a heart.
Take my word don't know a love.

21. Somebody (song)

Straight streets he walks alone
No direction, displeased some
Within heart a ray of hope
Somebody will come
Innocent he is people said
Empty hearted, sin free
Day will come
Somebody will see
O_ unique he is
Quite cheer and heal
Perhaps soon
Somebody will feel
No friends no company
Stepped down as to stream
About him
Somebody will dream
Rendering and wondering
Over seaside and cove
Firm faith
Somebody will love
Burnt nights, lost dreams
Who snatched his gay?

And sigh and murmured
Somebody will pray
Strange imaginations he pass
Sweet pain unseen lust
Still believe
Somebody will trust
Dizzy days they were
Freshening and fluttering he miss
When gazed setting sun
Somebody bliss
Nothing all his love in vain
With eyes upturn
Sky, moon, stars, learn
Somebody in burn

22. Four words

Who created me, why?
Behold such through blood in veins
How come to absurd sight that to my mind still
To be born as fairest May to the shades of age old grey
And to the dark that by dark death we call
Bear the brunt of soul to take me down to sleep
Why die, why die at all?
Has done this to us, why?
But not mathematician, am I? Numbers big I do know
To death so they can't escape how big doth let go
Multiplication that ends through death
Strength of beneath that no title cares
A big house holder once, mysteries of her grave
Dawn with blanket clay, and clay with clay, that mine
Long I work hard day and night to depart then
What is the meaning of life-it is not worth living
Hath I died in womb apart there possible worlds
Like the present one except for essence of eternity
Dust created from, a mixed drop
Some forces keep me driving
Source of which four words lie
Deeds, clock, livelihood, and hereafter that

Where do I find homeland in far off space
Leaves in autumn and days of May run by the clock
Oft in the yard to the pit of punishment
Or the garden of fruits seven beds of more bright

23. Stranger

I am not a stranger, who I am
I am a phenomenon worth seeing
See it again and again
I am but with that star
With no bright
That is where dead are

24. Take a look in the mirror

Take a look in the mirror
Into your memories, Into your thoughts
Into your present ,Into your past
Somehow I am there awake
Forgotten-But you know him well
As moon knows to gloom
As spring knows to bloom
Take a look in the mirror
For your beauty to make
Eyes and brows and arrows
And smile-would had took Him long
I know not-All that I know her voice
As smiling water falling down
As crystal stream wearing crown
Take a look in the mirror
Your past is but a silver coating
Painted to the same mirror
Reflecting me in front of
Break it or lash it, pieces will reflect but me
As desolation of rainbow

As sunrays behind the shadow
Take a look in the mirror
And feel the same last rainfall
Out me and you and you and me
Thunders and showers that our canopy
Whenever it is rainfall, your eyes tears will fall
As clouds bring to fading flower
As last spoken words of forgotten lover
Take a look in the mirror
In cold shiver winter nights
Somehow I am there awake and alive and
Take a look in the mirror
In the summer colourful days-I am there
As warm days are long
As birds singing a love song

25. The Tenth Mohhram

Stars and sky wept
For that sorrow I kept
As I look up this today
Empty, void, blood and grey
Lost son, daughter in pain
Pray for them to regain
I —cry I do not know
I see pain inside, it hurts me so
Deep sorrow this day behold
Silent mother, young and old
Day will come again and again
Hath history of truth and pain
There is no lecture, This is no class
Remember Him, while drinking a water of glass
I gave you tears for drinking
I gave you tears for drinking

26. The Game

A toy thereby in Mighty hands
One of a baby - A day dreamer
Doth know Sweet fancies such do last?
A saddle just put on back
Hanging stir up of years
Hopes that strikes with hoof
Doth mean rider on track
But if one of His bridle to gain
Let then rider in game -A race
The gift to end
With fragile and frail would have to stay
For one hath no wishes, no wants, and no finish
Burn hopes that rise
For one hath no wolf living inside
Aware not of sharp-eyed bad blood beings
What of chances - A Gullible one
Now but of his tricks and schemes
Waves that progress infinite with ups and downs
Oft whistles deep pattern of twists and turns
Make abstruse of level where contrite lie
Finally is winner of the game
Bedevil yourself, be devil outside

27. A black dog

A black dog-That is the difference, who am I
A loyal guardian to my master for I can die
I wake up all night for some food and piece of bone
And you eat up all life hunting, His kingdom and throne
I am the one who eat rotten, ripe, and dead and decay
And now you eat the same whatever it takes away
I always stand at the same door
For some bread, tasty or sour
I have no class, no civilization and position
But yours is to slit the throat, of your religion?
I don't believe in relations, marriage system
Same is you who lost their wisdom
Then father and mother I don't care who they are
Tell me, do you pay the visit whether near or far?
I am but a black dog with four legs I go for walk
What is it proud, for with two legs you walk?

28. Island of love

East and west and from heaven above
Rendering and circling island of love
Of well built nest of pure aspiration
Dreams But fly away to unknown destination
So am I in the age of kites and vultures
That swallow alive innocents and cultures
Days under wings of darkling
Ruled by threat of prince- charming
Call it age or call it cage
Where rich damage poor pay wage
Flowers die before they fall
Where moths flutter for life at all
Frozen tears instead of pearls
Where life is all about uncertain curls
And nights in desert half alive kept
Then by the left side where is that soft left?

29. Look again

As hearts being soft, angels and beasts doth like same end
Look again into your heart that once on mine, beat depend

The winged creatures do fly to others that to new heart
Of kings and riches of the world, expert in the art

For loving the beast is the love , what kind of?
Love to have no, the loved one's back, is just a laugh

To be a fragrant with pretty patterns of love, doth smell policy
Do they? Do they not? Both eat him pieces with no mercy

Of what material hearts are made oft?
Where outlooks seem-not crude and black smiles soft!

30. Once more into the battle

Once more into the battle. . .
Into the battle of life, I never blame
Into the battle of sorrow, I never overcame
Into the battle of illusion, I never heard
Into the battle of solitary, I never preferred
Like a child I
Walk alone
Rendering and wondering
Destination unknown
Why?
Why should I pass by?
Why should I fight battle?
Why could not my mind settle?
Looking around
Desert of emotion
That beautiful bird
With no commotion
To celebrate
There is no colorful day
Lost in brooding

No company and way
Wild winds calling his name
Fast loud and mean
Unhappy sky and
No sun to seen
No April rain, no days of gain
Caged bird in empty room
Autumn's sign
No flowers bloom
No falling leaves
No warm July
Oh warm days
No aircraft fly
No caterpillars, No butterfly

31. Gone by some autumn afternoon

Gone by some autumn afternoon
That I had never hoped to stand
Where of naked body sickening oft rages down
With you gone by some autumn afternoon winds
My love-then I stop loving and waving
But shed leaves and tears apart
Upon the golden, yellow and on pale face
Gently, she was gone like a white lily of spring
Morning rose, lifeless moth and
Birds but none flutter about branches
And sing no song such loneliness lie
Deep into the heart for it knows nothing but chill and frost
But love, for I- would hold her hand and
Sang her song in sweetest tone
Wrecked life once seems no wrong
Instead of busy bee shall I whisper to the wind
Of autumn afternoon that care not the hopes
That you would come again after the fall of night
And bring joyous time of warm sun
And presents gloom from the chest of cloud

Into the careless heart of a beast
Fears none, not the black heart of dawn
Oh-gone by some autumn afternoon
The day make the young silent soon
As own voiceless image cold and mute
As if the dark and the sun were not alive
Surprised me with shivering owl sat on same branch
Had hardly learnt to hoot all blue night long with me
I shed my leaves, I am half alive
This young bird that of distress
Oh-gone by some autumn afternoon
Dissolved roots into black clay of past
And grieves gently did pass said
Long time it may and not easy to breathe
As it is not spring , red and colorful road
Cold it is and owl and me
Blinking not from feet to feet in shiver wild
Gone by some autumn afternoon
Have I not met country folks once amaze
Those honey waxen-comb bees, but
Tangled web of fierce and spoil around
It raged the body, bloodless petals and feet
While unfold neck, strange smile owl passed
Hopes gone by some autumn afternoon asked
With flock once I was circling mountains and farms
Not naked but homes from bough to bough made
Noise, chirp, tones, songs, from the tree

I could almost see colors from the heaven above
Gone by some autumn afternoon
Washed body upon the trunk and I
Stand in chills waiting spring times that are
Gone by some autumn afternoon

32. Wish

Life is getting darker
No single sign you leave behind
No peace ,no direction
And do not know where to find

As life do not last forever
Now, then, today, tomorrow
I will leave and never come back
And you'll enjoy my sorrow

Darkness covered all over the sky
Watching my own eye
Hope _you'll come
And eyes thirst but nights cry

Search you every nook and corner
Mountain, plain, hill, meadow
Search you everywhere I can
Can't find even your shadow

One day I will die I will be lost
I have a wish
Before I go
Before I perish

That you'll look my way
Not enough I have to say
Cause I'm alone in universe
All I think is about yours

Come back to me…come back
Trust me your companion and guard
Come back in my life
Else! You'll find me in graveyard.

33. I could fly again

Then in the distant horizon but
Sunless sky, no creep around
How far the bright
When that bright?
As such the clouds heavy do hang
Never dies into the rain
The warm hours of spring
Sharp drifting of soft behave
Blooms, yellow bees, fragrant bough
High up the touch of wilderness
Soft tones and voices die
Blooms and moths cry
Autumn of my life
Where is soft violet clear moon?
That I gazed and fall asleep
The woods and the dense?
That I woke with my friends
I smiled upon silent tree
And care the frozen to free
Muted bird and the neck
Turned round
Far away from flock dejected by

ABID MASROOR SHAH

To the gardens and busy towns
To the ups and stream downs
Falls and fountains
Top of mountains
Free to be myself
Wish I could fly again

34. Beautiful creature

The unwilling forces no dark to surprise
As bright the side when by my side
If by the thunder high, laugh I pass
Blessed enough perfect wind on my side
Smooth things – O smiling silent sail
But the tide-motion which made
Moon and starry sky almost to fall
Let them go and I slow down
Alone sink with souls of winter
And float across the un-reposing wave
And now, with distance of spring
Let you go with new paths of hope
But take my word O beautiful creature
When in the season of rose bloom
The awful silence of the bright full -moon
While from lips the forgotten words
Then again would wake and arise

35. Snowfall

Here once again I'm alone
Scared, fearsome by fickle cold
I put the faggot and glance at the fire
Sit beside with little admire
Outside the window, sun is murdered
Slow windward, clean sheet and dim light
At the vastness of white
Snowfall throughout this night
Stiffness and cold in air
Gently falling, floating down
I put on scarf and glove
As flakes are falling from heaven above
Oh snowfall in the moonlight
Like a child I walk happily
Making sounds in silent snowy night
Silence of the night is winter's delight
Not even single creature creeps
Out in wooded forest hallow
Let the trees and moonlight sing
Let the snow and cold wind bring

36. The floating cloud

In the universe of amaze
Sky of mist, stars of list
Like a cloud I was
Rendering for, for no cause
I fly high up in the air
See and imagine, imagine what I could
Harsh, odd, void, rare delight
Month of blossom, snowfall in sunlight
Though I passed the barren lands
No pleasant image of care
cliff of loneliness
Hug of void, call it darkness
Like an oasis she was
No matter life is an empty vessel
Seems battle of dreams will end soon
Dregs of life, call it moon
With stars her calm family
Silent sympathy she behold
And for her I —the floating cloud
Distant horizon fluttering loud

37. WHY

I am the man, always confounded in questions
Why this, why that, why suggestions
Why now, why not now, why here
Why there, why fear, why tear
Why sky looks blue
Why some questions needs clue
Why billows came from cloud
Why thunders are loud
Why they cross the sky
Why I cannot fly
Why stars should shine
Why beauty is like a divine
Why sun sets behind the hills
Why single word sometime kills
Why people are with superiority ego
Why we are put down as a foe
Why cast, why creed, why color
Why life comes up with different flavor
Why birth is celebration, why death is sorrow
Why today is today why not tomorrow
Why boundary, why border, why barrier
Why every year we loosing great warrior

Why our hands are blood dyed
Why hearts are black inside
Why bisection, why bifurcation
Why everyone is in misconception
Knowing all the reasons of "WHY"
Why am I asking...WHY?

38. Why me?

Of the wide world many things around
But my love fresh upon my heart
Of false I had lived
The love to bear, heavy trend
Her pretty looks being foe not friend
What I seek not ease climate for sail
Frown , frozen and tossed by the waves of life
Wound not me with your eyes, smile and face
But if with true words of slain
Teardrops greet me but would have short pain
Clouds that settle with your love
Tides that raise my thoughts
Perhaps bring an eclipse, oh my sweet fancies
Why me? The journey with buried sun
Rise again what is already run
On counting two lives I do have
Two are things divided as humans
As from mind two stages lie
Why me? Love stepped down most low
What your heart hath, not seem so
Time that keeps you in my chest
Without which not even survive

Therefore love for love is rare
Why me? Swift waves, feather love I been
Float wherever black hearts are seen

39. The night among woods

I breathe one after another
Among the dark dense woods
Among the pine
Where no one I am sure must be
Where waves, scent of wild should be
Where there is
Me, myself and my soul
With a solitary heap with little goal
Where there is no love
No currents of heart would arise
No life of care but heaven
Nor presence of creature around
How lost in wild amaze
No swift cloud to fly with
But sudden from above a weeping cloud
Would burst tears stream and loud
No moon to gaze a little
To taste the sorrow of her
As if murdered by noon
Ah-moonless night

Favorable night to the wild and tide
No sun bright stations to climb
Chained sunny land
Blue or violet or both
No matter how cold it is, I like both
Where
Flowers behaving that undeserving way
As if spring has sudden changed to winter
Moths dissolved in rain
The winds, opposite
To their nests and so to me
My eyes grow colder, wet and free
Blink of lightning, thunder of rain
Touch and Wash away my pain
I could almost smell days of gold
The golden sight that never sets
Shall I deep myself or shall I low
Shall I stay on or shall I go

40. Autumn and Me

Mark the cold, mute and
Naked tree erect
Point out the season?
Pain reflect
Had left all
Dark paths of eerie
And mark in that
Cold mind of freeze
Where is that faithful breeze?
Oath sunshine and fruitful trees
Is that I am still erect and alive
Is that I shouldn't be?
Like a Twig of blossom
In twilight blunder
Rain of pain
In shower of thunder
My body —sack of bones, broken sap
In that observe
The shivery and gap
I am not alive and awake
Ask the
Falcon-the witness of gale

Little nook in hay of bale
Had left all about me
I am down and let me be
Let the winter blanket for me
Let the spring hope for me
Let the summer burn for me
Let the autumn balm for me

41. A Dream

The soft sky smiles when I opened my eye
Bright new day and the land is gone
I wake up my crew wide open and calm
Gentlemen —world is deep since this is none
Whether they lose, we gain in this
Perfect time wind equal low
And reason far, down below feet lie
Tie every hook and rope
Follow every nook and rope
Cause today we going rich
Ropes? Yes Captain...
Bait? Almost done captain...
We good to go
Work on such length of hours
Knock the hearing a moment took
That sea in middle is wild
Blind the brain, fold the heart
From which no sailor returns
The middle of lost souls
But nothing compares to the vast see
Loud whooshing- wind whistling and I
Gentlemen- we have a new course

THE WILDFIRE.

Listen to the wind
It is unfavorable
And to the clattering – to death
Prepare as she goes
All hands to trusses
Free the covers
Cut the main rope
And pray to the God? We may need Him
Proud for me been fishing with you
And wait for my command...
Time to go home- move
It is 9 AM look out the window- wake up
Sunny bright Sunday it is- mommy?

42. I go to Kashmir

Love the way you love the rain
Not enough to show the pain
May be clouds are not with you
Up to HIM lose or gain

Winds will blow through your ear
World will make you thousand fear
This is true my dear
That good atmosphere is rare

Everywhere scenes of false filled
Month of blossom killed
Season of moths asperse
Flock of birds disperse

Dreams of baby in vain
Mother and sister in pain
Sighs instead of song
Kashmir-Guilt, dark, wrong

Same are the mountains here
Same people with no cheer
Stones, bullets, blood dyed hand
Caged bird in beautiful land

Paradise on earth
We call it land of birth
They say blooming buds are here and I
Fighting, struggling, heart filled with no fear

43. I am me

Through tough have I passed
Too weak to gather it
Dry, hard, chill and dead
Always bouncing inside my head
Like a child my mind hit
Have no idea where had I come
Full of false filled with
Acting as, it is a myth
I am innocent people said
Empty hearted sin free
I am a programmer
Good in syntax and grammar
I am a perfect man
Quite cheer and heal
Fair look, haired with gold
Deep blue eyes I behold
Yes In the rain of sorrow I
Walk straight streets alone
No direction, displeased some
For me the day will come
Live my life simple
Found lost myself in

THE WILDFIRE.

Classes, loops, iterations and functions
I live outside, free of tensions
I live myself comfortable life
Programming my girlfriend, laptop my wife
Whenever she doesn't mail
I die, I cry, and I fail

44. A computer

Void, empty, null, hallow
Lost in one's and zero's
In world alone and apart
Trying to execute Restart
Yes my software tools that missing
Programs —but make rebooting
Circuits and gates how to be prepared
I know not how it can be repaired
Alone to face nightmares
Alone to face bugs
Alone to face new hardware
Alone to face new software
Interrupts —come and go away my dear
There is nothing to fear
But no one see my deadlock
Broken address bus, pulse and clock
And there is no one to mend it
Run- but how, in halt state
All the data lost away
All the buffers betray
Debuggers , compilers , linking modes
Control flow and clear roads

THE WILDFIRE.

45. One more chance (Song)

O – Killer could not forget you

Hurt me, not once

Yes everywhere is your presence

Give me one more chance

Give me one more chance

Seasons are changing

Melt snow melt

Vast greenery, Beautiful scenery

Birds sing and dance

Give me one more chance

Give me one more chance

Solid mountains, Blue the vast sky

All over I see butterflies and flowers by

Dizzy moves, pleasant fragrance

Give me one more chance

Give me one more chance

Cloudless sky

Warm nights and I

In solitary nights, feeling your absence

Give me one more chance

THE WILDFIRE.

Give me one more chance
Full moon nights –In candle lights
Silent snowy nights-cool breezy sights
Day dreaming and severance
Give me one more chance
Give me one more chance

46. I am gone

I am gone for let me be
Into the deep, wide sea of misery
Of vast and illusive shore
My lines are down, never before
Act comfort on the odds of bay
Oh-day and night and night and day
I am gone and my voyage
Unfavorable winds in cheerless age
And in all this tempest track
I am down with my heart- dark and black
Let me see on the river bank
Till the ship has almost sank
I am gone let it rain over me
Perish-let there only be me
With the tides of sea
With dark, deep, careless and cold
That something my love would fold
I am gone —a few last stand
Into the water of wide- no land
No earth to rebirth, no stars by near
No moon to gaze, no sun to care
What if I am in the afternoon?

And autumns delight meets me soon
Such things silly and goon
I am gone let the autumn sail constant motion
Dream indeed imaginary ray in the dark ocean
Welcome him with inner emotion
Floating body with little commotion
I am gone let me with waves forever
To learn and observe sorrow of river
As I now behold myself here
Would imagine things, never there were
Say for me this is a curse
YES-but I would say not worse
No matter how waves descend me down
let me with autumn's crown
I am gone into the middle of way
Overcome-just grip the hope of ray

47. A girl and mid-night rains

The opposite nights
Undiscribed sound top of falling sky
The pretty haired girl of village and her beauty
Unseen —as are unseen her lips-a story behold
Live once again that mid-night rainfall with flowers and moths
down
With the pattern, with the past, with the falling drops
On muted hillocks on monsoon crops

Poor heart but pour the heart that not a mysteries of fall
I cannot smile pages to unlock
Neither can I weep and melt my path
Smile and smell what it looks up in fragrant flowers that dwell
On road of life when will be it the last steep and cliff

I dare to fall
Then let window open, of heart and of mind, the door
O sweet starless sky

Let the raindrops fall on my face ,ahh this pain
Bubble of life burst soundless and my loss
That of pain let you loose and the same tell me?
How many nights when moon doth see gloom
And eyes go fade
To the wintery how frozen and frost to pass
And full moons how let go?

48. Alone

Island-in an ocean of tears
I am single, alone and my fears
Which to repair is but huge frozen wall
With natures gift sunlight in snowfall
Then what could death do when I depart
And when there is empty chamber of heart
Hath no fear to loose, no one to recall
Hath no pains to choose, no deserving to fall
Ask the whispering drifts of breeze
Am I alone in cold days of freeze?
They say I am idol of solidity
When I have kissed the forehead of difficulty

THE WILDFIRE.

49. Best fit

Right from first semester I
Was in waiting queue
Hope she will execute
No scheduling, not even user view
Though
I wait and check my process
Good interface, good synchronization
Good time slot, good allocation
And was good hardware implementation
So
What makes me deadlock?
What makes me prevention?
Who interrupted my life cycle?
What makes me starvation?
Am i. . .
Multiprocessing as like as you?
Multiprogrammed as like as you?
Multitasking like as you?
Multithreaded like as you?
No. . .
I was the best fit
Not even single page fault

THE WILDFIRE.

First in race condition
Why in state of halt?
Answer is. . .
All we have is priority problem
Selection mode, loving nerve
And how could I forget the, Algo
First come first serve

50. Desert Of Emotions

Then I went to the vale of love
Upturn my head to vast sky
Yon bluish hue is burned
Loud, wild, tempestuous winds
Blow through my ears
Restless clouds lost their direction
Jollity of myself come to an end

Through the darkness and cold I
See the stars in twinge
And rare twinkle in twilight gloom
That crescent moon
Sly gazing at me
My heart sighs
Went back to
Lines, words, sentences, verses
Went back to
The fields of solitary
Cliff of loneliness
Forests of thoughts

THE WILDFIRE.

Desert of emotions
Oceans of sighs And
I wrote a song
People listen curious
Named me "Keats"
A romantic poet

51. Goodnight

Ending of September harvest, with setting sun
Deep golden rays scattered, fall on my face
Far in wide open fields yellow and gold
Folk song almost lower tune hold
When west mountain see him silent hours
To the same I waved arms open
Among the mountain farm wild
Evening stars began mother's cuddle her child
Short my day was and the sun is gone I
Lie round on mother when limbs did bend
Another day! Another unfinished daily task
Of catching caterpillars, and stay near to ask
All flitting birds returned
Little joy heart of peace, how low clear song of her
In that I heard the blessing to you to me to all
Same kiss on cheek before I fall
Mind when sinking deep
Hands clench to the same her hair that I grasp
In candle-light of solitary window in calm of twilight
Moonlight, stars of midnight spoke to me goodnight!

52. Kashmir

The land this wide home of love paradise I call
Happiest region sweeten by the spring spot of clouds
Same with days white April sky
O sweet my blooms and buds
It never had lived in love lot, they say
A place of love, care, fountains, streams
Where from above fall
Snows are soul of all
But none compare beauties of world
To the same in moonlight, in the wildest woods apart
Between cloud and sun
A game of hide and seek were seen
And hawks and winds play
That I have not given away

53. Love lines

Inclines- how much yet have I, to qualify long

Can I, but how to make, towards the inconstancy wrong

I smile and live sincerely there, I have gone,

From your memories and heart, I do not belong

Would that I have died before this life

Or tell the same what man hopes, where arrogance is rife

Hearts slaughtered there with careless knife

This syndrome is full of strife

How I wish you would come back again tomorrow

In spring to bring sound to my heart and that glow

Ahh- my winter nights grow longer with grief's and sorrow

When days I recall, we spent together tears will flow

I go from spring to autumn because of loving you

From white angel to black beast, to create me new

I go from thinking to not thinking ,about you

From beautiful stations to the only place I knew

Shadows, my love —You played with eyes so wild

Games and tricks in your mind, like played with a child

That describe distances, with changes warm and mild

Gone from your memories, from deep eyes that smiled

54. Mother and Son

Mother lookout-Again that bird has come
To repeat the same old tones, rueful some
In the dry, on the naked leafless tree
I do not know, why it is obscure to me

" That female bird lost brother in winter storm
That she cries out when snow cloud took form "
What is it- this repetitive tone , I asked my mother?
It is chirping note "Come back to me my little brother"

" A black story beholds this white snow
Some enjoy, some do not, very few know "
Mother-For little bird I should pray
That dry winds come, to blow her pain away

" How good it is-My little cub, love to all
Who pity the weak and small ,they never fall
Come home inside ,it will snowfall tonight
Be prepare ,here I am ready for snow fight"

Mother- I will make big snowball then I will throw
And we will go far, trace footsteps in the snow
" My little boy-And who will built a snowman?
You will try alone-But together we can "

Mother -I would love to ski with- fire in the pot
" Ski with pot, son-That make it wrong, I think not
But scarf and glove, you can wear, that I weave
And promise me, you will never lie and deceive "

" World there is so cruel and mean-My dear son
Beware of new false faces wherever you begun "
Mother-I am brave, I must be careful then?
My little cub-,like you-out there are, very few men

Mother-where is moon, I will marry moon
Let her not pass away till next day at noon!!!
" They don't marry son because they are very far
But surely can, if you are the brightest star "

" From some old marvelous tale I have read

Dark souls never become a star-they said
And within every heart two angels behold
It is only good one can make it against the cold "

Mother-can angels fly
From hearts ,into the sky
Watch us —from heaven above high
Thereby are they alive, do they die?

" My little man- your intensions and actions
God in heaven will be laughing on your questions
When you grow up vision so broad
Give thanks and ask same to the lord "

" Now it is time for bed-tale
Once there was a ship, began to sail"
Mother-what happened to the little bird
She cries out notes ,her brother never heard?

55. A dialogue between a bird and me

When in the midst of river
As open in the autumn shiver
I sit down upset and smoke
From the distance of little folk
Thereby in the silence a song I heard
And somewhere I saw a singing bird

" Say something 'O' you Hunter?
What makes you upset and thunder
Is it? seems all around His mystery
Then He made it with grave and uncertainty
Is it? you are lost in two's
Then in between you have to choose
Is it? you lost the dearest one
Then it is ,how it is done
Is it? the mean and evil leads
Then He loves testing good deeds
Is it? the love syndrome
Then bend over towards His throne

Is it? the winter, the summer or moon
Then look at me my days are June. "

No, little bird-Hunter but, I am not
And now, I do not- what I forgot
I saw lofty trees began to fade
Beneath the branches no afternoon shade
Full blooms but in vain
Rose and lily weep and rain
Clouds they don't bring for thirsty
But dissolve in smoke and dirty
There is no snowfall
No chill, no ski and no snow-ball

I saw April dead blossoms and bough
Men now, they don't follow the plough
Oaks and moths ,grass and worms
Buried into void by blood storms
I saw sun from December to May
I saw April enjoying holiday
Say something 'O' you little bird
What makes now you absurd?

" I live in woods, my family and friend

It once was where sorrows end
A place like heaven where all my kin
Fly and played before men came in
To cast shadows, my nest ,my woody land
I wash their blood with my own hand

Bats, butterflies, bulbul our world is mute
Owls gone ,midnights and moonlights, no hoot
For my woody land men killing men
Tell us the same where to go then? "

We call it civilization
Where there is exploitation
We call it modernization
Where there is no plantation
There was a time we used to get together
Wintery nights with family and grandmother
Around candle light to listen her old fairy tale
Kings, knights, horses, warriors, wars, and vale
Silent cold nights are gone
So is Autumn River wandering on

56. To Grandma

Don't you leave me, for I know not
How to live it, because days and nights
And nights and days are long
I am melting because of you
Go waiting for you, from dawn to dusk
My heart is blue and frozen
Because of you, because I do not know
How to live it, in flowers ,in glooms, in blooms
'O' spring has come again,
Come for me, somewhere from your grave
Because I do not know how to
Recover, rebuilt and repair my heart
I have loved but you, O beautiful white lady
Come for me, wake up and resuscitate
Because I do not know how to
Lend my shoulder and dry my tears
Because I do not know how to
Conquer fears and wrongs and evils
There is no one to watch me play
And no one to feed me with tricks
Your smiles, your stories, your songs
Say my name again and hold my hand

Because I do not know,
My arms are empty and void
Hugs, kisses, advises, surprises
You mean the world to me
O let me walk with you, for your footsteps
Are short as are mine
O let me see with you, for your eyes
See as mine do
O let me sleep with you, for you
Are my good morning and good night
Active and surprise
O let me work with you, for you
Are a garden lover
O let me dream with you
Because you're a best story teller
And laughter and writer and a good kisser
O let me be with you
Because I do not know, how to
Love, because I love you
Let me be with you,
Because I love to make your hair-knot
O let me sit and weep on your grave
With your scent, with your grass

57. Goodbye grandma

Goodbye-O my land

Goodbye to you where I stand

To you O grandma and your grave

Where flowers and lily wave

To you O sweet busy bees

To you O blossom, bough, and trees

Goodbye everyone

Stars, moon morning sun

Goodbye my beautiful lady

I am grown but man from little baby

58. For His Mother

September morning with its secrets
Is in progress, so am I
Trying to find the new hope
The crops, and the trees
Favorite walnuts, yellow fields and same winds
As if autumn winds
Unquiet and unseen blows for cause and change
Into the blue, into the green, into the vale
But skies and souls weep, break and fall
Men and women, women and men
Red are buds with your fragrance,
This September
Where are the farmers?
I am trying to find the being
Because being is the being of beings and
To be is to be related
Sigh that speak of love
Of beauty, Of sweetness, Of peace and pattern
Where are the busy bees?
This September
The breeze not so very calm and cool and close
Dreams as well as dove are gone

And so is saddened woman's son
If to be is to be related
What makes it graveyards fill?
If to be is to be related, then
Man has no power to kill
Because he is not All-powerful,
Eternal , unlimited, mighty at all,
As we all come from beings
What we encounter are all beings
A dark night fall on my face
September O September wait a while
Let the leaves catch the breath
Let the winds slow down
Cry not, sisters and mothers
For I will there stand for you
For hope ,hope of tomorrow
And if, this is a crime
I will commit it again and again
And if, I got a bullet in my chest
Mother, to be is to be related
Ashes with ashes, dust with dust

59. Half love

You could be anytime- victimized,
Terrorized, traumatized, brutalized by the
Experience of being in love
love? But I am not a cup, a coffee, a cupboard, a curtain
For hearts and curtains are very thin material, love
One can't prevent them from seeing in
What is happening?
What is it wrong I have done? that
If hundred years, I look at you
If hundred miles, I wait but you
If hundred smiles, I choose you
Such a hopeless in love but
It is written in the winds
"Lesser my hope harder my love"
And I have only just begun
Loved but you,
Not in wonderland's and Disneyland's
In every season, in every year, in every autumn
In snowfalls, in rainy days, in Junes in Mays
In full moons ,in glooms
Men and women and women and men
Both fall in love

Die for love, kill for love
Sing for love,
Compose poems in love
Some of them fall for romantic love
Some of them fail for romantic love
And some get rejected ,some dumped in love
For world without love is a deadly place
No morality, no sentiment
Filled with voracity and wolfishness
But love, my love is
Inert, Immotile, irremovable,
Permanent, stagnant, unmovable,
Calm, frozen, halted, paralyzed,
As in the age of means
Who would huddle to hear tales of fairies
Moonlit nights and love songs
These things here exist not
You could find a great man more easily
Superior and supreme of a very high standard
Who can buy rings and earrings
Etcetera etcetera
Where you look but not for me at all
And sure this half love of yours, be gone
For I know women very well
She is good in decisions and demands and duality
How can I define myself?
I no longer have any fear of death

I am half alive, half dead
I am a beast ,a demon
Demonized by the chains that bind you
I am a raptor, very good at noticing things
What then doubt and fear?
I am a survivor where one dies, and one lives
Cauterized by risk, prisons and walls
I am a failure,
Failed in winning life's greatest prize
Year by year as the years pass
Do slowly finish this half, my love
For mine shall always glitter like a star,
Wrinkled somewhere in the corner

60. Born in Mid April

Gone up in the attic oft
Mountain pores and love gardens aloft
Trails of floras and daffodils are resuscitated in hilly
Irresistible call to butterflies, and plantain lily
Long white war done, no tyranny more authority
On heavenly pines and oak, on living dead majority
Because winter had to pass by
It changes winds but not the sky
Lost battle not the war
From the same field and scar
Water oozed in place of blood
Not spring, not leaf- not a bud
Love; brought them back to life again
But born in mid April, is occasional gain
And I haven't seen anything aesthetic in my squad
Her Patel's , Patterns, Body - God!!!
To men give them another heart
For attacks and strokes they fall apart
By some old sacred text, the flower is remedy
Cure to illnesses and injury
Symbol of love, romantic
Musing to and fro by some platonic

61. Half-done

This summer of all midst this dwell

Winds, bestrew no sense of smell

From the same I saw glimmer of the setting sun

Pointing to the moon that "my days are done"

And when I asked the moon

Her glow faded in the month of June

The white so bright calm moonlight

Once bare bosom to the summer tide

Not a whit of love, I no longer catch the scent

Birds and bulbul are long absent

What hearts made but of yowl

Bees , Blossom, Moths and an Owl

Give another hoot of a new mourning song

Hush and cry! this cold night long

Under the starry sky beneath the cove

For half slaughtered casualties of love

And upon the branch of fractured tree

Once chosen used to be

Indistinct tonight ,my grave of beloved one

It must be love; half-done

"We smoke too much,

talk too much,

laugh with friends that too much,

walk little, eat too much,

we love, we hate

get angry too much,

we read, we write

we got skills too much,

we work, we play

we sleep too much,

waste our time that too much,

we fail, we learn,

we get back into our business,

we run, we fight, we multiply, we die,

we risk our lives

we are good in making livings

but not the civilization, society,

culture, mother-tongue and our religion

no matter we came into being from nothing and went back of

being nothingness

but to live is to earn, To earn is to learn

and to learn is to learn to die"

Abid Masroor.

Glossary

- ***Abstruse****: hard to understand, something whose meaning is hidden,*
- ***Askance****: look at something or someone with suspicious or distrust.*
- ***Aye****: always.*
- ***Agape****: Greek word which means love, especially brotherly love or the love of God for man and of man for God.*
- ***Admire****: to regard with wonder, pleasure, or approval, to feel respect.*
- ***Asperse****: to attack with false, evil, malicious, and damaging charges or insinuations .*
- ***Awful****: very bad or unpleasant.*
- ***Algo****: used for algorithm in this content.*
- ***Bale:*** *a large ,bound quantity of hay.*
- ***Bliss:*** *perfect happiness, great joy, reach a state of perfect happiness, obvious of every thing else*
- ***Bait:*** *food or other lure placed on a hook or in a trap and used in talking of fish ,birds or animals.*
- ***Brittle:*** *hard but easily broken.*
- ***Baffle****: prevent from doing something.*
- ***Bereavement****: a great loss, lacking deprived of.*
- ***Beware****: be on guard, be aware of danger.*
- ***Bridle****: the headgear used to control a horse, consisting of buckled straps to which a bit or reins are attached.*

- ***Bough***: *a main branch of a tree.*
- ***Bedevil***: *of something bad ,throw into disorder, cause continual trouble to*
- ***Brooding:*** *think deeply about an, think long and sadly on or upon something.*
- ***Blaze:*** *something already make it known far and wide, make known widely, fire guns quickly*
- ***Clench***: *grip, close tightly*
- ***Contrite***: *fitted with deep sorrow for sin, feeling or expression remorse at the recognition that one has done wrong.*
- ***Cliff***: *a steep rock face ,especially at the edge of sea*
- **Canopy**: *a cloth held up over a throne or bed.*
- ***Cheer***: *shout for joy or to praise or encourage.*
- ***Conscience***: *a person's moral sense of right and wrong, viewed as acting as a guide to ones behavior.*
- ***Creep***: *to move slowly with the body close to the ground ,as reptile or an insect, or a person on hands and knees.*
- ***Creed***: *a system of religious belief.*
- **Cuddles:** *hug lovely, lie or sit close.*
- ***Commotion***: *mental excitement .*
- ***Crude:*** *rough or vulgar.*
- **Confound**: surprise.
- **Corpse**: *a dead body.*
- ***Deadlock***: *situation where two or more processes are waiting for resource in a circular chain, it is a technical term in computer science, in operating systems.*
- ***Doth***: *do not.*

- **Coagulate**: *thickening of liquid or become semi solid.*
- **Distress**: *pain or hardship.*
- **Dire**: *very serious or urgent , very bad.*
- *Disperse*: *distribute or spread over a wide area.*
- *Drift*: *go slowly and aimless.*
- *Doom*: *death or another terrible fate.*
- *Drove:* *force to move, forward, to, away, out, into, through, on.*
- *Dubious*: *doubtful, not clear*
- *Divine*: *addressed, appropriated, or devoted to God.*
- *Dregs:* *drink to dregs, worst and useless part.*
- **Downpour**: *a heavy rainfall.*
- *Eerie*: *strange and frightening, causing a feeling of fear or mystery.*
- **Exploitation**: *treat or use unfairly.*
- **Eclipse**: *an occasion when one planet, moon etc blocks out the light from another.*
- *Emit*: *discharge, send out.*
- **Embrace**: *hold closely in one's arms as a sighn of affection.*
- *Fierce*: *powerful ,violent, aggressive, very cruel.*
- *Faggot*: *a bundle of fire wood. sticks tied together as fuel.*
- *Flutter*: *move with a light trembling motion.*
- *Frown:* *furrow one's blows in an expression indicating disapproval, displeasure, or concentration*
- *Flit:* *move quick and lightly.*
- *Flown*: *past participle of fly.*
- *Fanatically*: *fanatical comes from word fanatic, which itself came from the Latin fanaticus , meaning "mad" the word fanatically in this context means madly.*

- ***Foe***: *a person who feels enmity, hatred, or malice towards another.*
- ***Falsities***: *the fact of being untrue, incorrect, or insincere.*
- **Fancies**: *imagine think.*
- **Fickle:** *changeable, mood or weather.*
- **Frazzle**: *an exhausted state.*
- ***Fragile***: *easily broken or damaged, delicate*
- ***Frail*** *:weak, fragile.*
- ***Folk***: *people .*
- ***Firepot***: *name given to traditional "kangri".*
- ***Fade***: *lose or cause to lose colour.*
- ***Gale***: *a very strong wind.*
- ***Galaxies***: *a system of millions of stars, together with gas and dust held together by gravitational attraction.*
- ***Gaze***: *a look steadily and intently, a steady intent look*
- **Grieves**: *suffer or cause grief.*
- ***Guile***: *insidious cunning in attaining a goal, crafty or artful deception.*
- ***Gleaming***: *shine brightly, especially with reflected light.*
- **Glory**: fame and honour.
- ***Gullible***: *easily deceived, or easily persuaded to believe something, credulous.*
- ***Hue***: *a colour or shade*
- ***hoof***: *the horny part of foot of an ungulate animal, especially in horse.*
- ***Hotbed***: *a place where something grows or develops easily.*
- **Honour**: great respect.
- **Hoot**: *a low sound made by owls.*

- ***Hath***: *archaic third person singular present of have*
- ***Inglorious***: *disgraceful, shameful.*
- ***Idol***: *an image false or representation of god.*
- ***Lofted***: *hit, kick.*
- ***Mingle***: *to combine or bring together two or more things ,meeting.*
- ***Moth***: *an insect like butterfly ,usually active at night.*
- ***Meadow***: *a field of grass.*
- ***Mist***: *a cloud or tiny droplets suspended in the atmosphere at or near the earths surface that limits visibility.*
- ***Nook***: *a corner or small place that is inside something.*
- **Nasty**: unpleasant, spiteful.
- ***Oath***: *a solemn promise, a swear word.*
- ***Oft***: *archaic or literary form of often.*
- ***Obscured***: *not known about or well known, hard to understand or see.*
- ***Pit of punishment***: *hell.*
- ***Pride***: *pleasure or satisfaction, self respect.*
- **Praise**: express approval.
- ***Paradoxes***:*a statement that seems to contradict itself but may infact be true.*
- **Perplex**: *great puzzle.*
- ***Rage***: *a violent anger . or uncontrollable anger.*
- **Rife**: *widespread.*
- ***Resurrection***: *restore to life, condition of having been restored to life.*
- ***Rueful***: *expressing sorrow.*
- ***Recast***: *give (a metal object)a different form by melting it down*

and reshape it.

- **Repose**: *a state of calm or peace.*
- **Roaming** *:move about or travel aimless or unsystematically, especially over a wide area.*
- **Severance**: *the action of ending a connection or relationship. the condition of being severed, separation, partition.*
- **Shill**: *an accomplice of a confidence trickster or swindler who poses as a genuine customer to entice or encourage others.*
- **Sely:** *innocent,*
- **Strife:** *bitter disagreement.*
- **Syndrome**: *a group of symptoms consistently occurring together.*
- **Shiver**: *shake slightly especially from fear or cold.*
- **Stir:** *a slight physical movement.*
- **Slain:** *kill a person or animal in violent way.*
- **Scent:** *a distinctive smell ,especially one that is pleasant.*
- **Saddle**: a seat on the back of horse for riding
- **Speck**: *atiny spot, mark with small spots*
- **Starvation**: *is a resource management problem where a process does not get the resource it needs for a long time because the resource are being allocated to other process, it is a term used in computer science.*
- **Simmer**: *be in a state of barely suppressed anger or excitement.*
- **Stalk**: *the main stem of a herbaceous plant.*
- **Scarce**: *insufficient for the demand*
- **Streaming**: *a flow of water in a channels or bed ,as a brook rivulet, or small river*
- **Synchronization:** *process of precisely coordinating or matching*

two or more activities, devices or processes in time.

- *__Treacherous__: guilty of involving betrayal or deception or having hidden dangers*
- *__Twig__: a slender woody shoot growing from a branch or stem.*
- *__Trusses:__ a framework typically consisting of rafters ,posts, and struts, supporting a roof ,bridge or other structure.*
- *__Thickets:__ a dense growth of shrubs ,or plants*
- *__Twilight__: when soft light from the sky when the sun is below the horizon.*
- *__Tempest__: a violent windstorm especially one with rain, hail, or snow.*
- *__Twinge__: a brief ,sharp or pang.*
- *__Tangle__: a twist into a confused.*
- *__Uprear__: raise up, lift up,*
- **Vale**: a valley.
- **Voyage**: *a long journey involving travel by sea.*
- **Void**: *empty, not valid, like an empty space.*
- *__Windward__: the side or direction from which the wind is blowing.*
- **Wrecked**: *the destruction of ship at sea.*
- *__Whooshing__: move quickly or suddenly with a rushing sound.*
- *__Whistle__: a clear ,high pitched sound .*
- **Woe**: sorrow or distress, trouble or misfortune.
- **Wage:** *a fixed regular payment for work.*
- *__Yon__: that.*

www.ingramcontent.com/pod-product-compliance
Lightning Source LLC
Chambersburg PA
CBHW020608160726
47991CB00002BA/679